MAKE ME LAUGH!

FOUL PLAY

JOKES THAT WON'T STRIKE OUT

by Rick and Ann Walton
pictures by Brian Gable

Carolrhoda Books, Inc. • Minneapolis

Q: What do basketball players do when they're happy?

A: Court-wheels.

Q: What football team can't swim?

A: The Oakland Waders.

Q: What are a basketball player's favorite flowers?

A: Guard-enias.

Q: Where do guards throw the guard-enias?

A: Into flower baskets.

Q: Why did the baseball player take a mitt to the beach?

A: To catch some rays.

Q: When did the Sun play baseball?

A: In the All-Star game.

Q: Why do happy ghosts play basketball?

A: Because they're high-spirited.

Q: Why do people like basketball players?

A: Because they are court-eous.

Q: What sport do thunderclouds like best?

A: Major Leak Baseball.

Q: What do the Oakland A's hit with?

A: Alpha-bats.

Q: What did the batter sing when the storm broke?

A: "I'm Swingin' in the Rain . . ."

Q: Which baseball players trot around the bases?

A: The Philadelphia Fillies.

Q: What do the Philadelphia Fillies eat?

A: The Oakland Hays.

Q: Who can start a fire by rubbing two baseball bats together?

A: A baseball scout.

Q: If a baseball field floods, how do the players get around?

A: In dugout canoes.

Q: What football team can really move the pigskin?

A: The Green Bay Porkers.

Q: Where do cows play foot-bull?

A: At the Super Bull.

Q: Who blows the whistle at foot-bull games?

A: The heiferee.

Q: Where do centers grow?

A: In center fields.

Q: What sport do cows like to play?

A: Foot-bull.

Q: What do basketball players put on their sandwiches?

A: Ball-oney.

Q: What do basketball players snack on?
A: Turnovers.

Q: Why do baseball coaches go to art museums?
A: To look for good pitchers.

Q: What sport do bakers like to play?

A: Biscuit ball.

Q: What did the referee give the quarterback?

A: A pig pen-alty.

Q: When pigs play baseball, what do they want to win?

A: The pig pen-nant.

Q: What do you get if a sick basketball player breathes on you?

A: Hooping cough.

Q: Why did the coach take away his players' credit cards?

A: To keep them from charging.

Q: What do you call a game between the Celtics and the Westside Elementary Fourth Grade All-Stars?

A: A Boston Massacre.

Q: What did the batboy want to be when he grew up?

A: Batman.

Q: What football player likes to spend money?

A: The shopping center.

Q: Where do batter-flies come from?

A: Batter-pillars.

Q: What's skinny, full of ink, and makes you lose fifteen yards?

A: A ballpoint penalty.

Q: What did the referee call when all the Philadelphia Eagles got sick and ran off the field?

A: Ill-Eagle motion.

Q: Why does the umpire brush off home plate?

A: It's his homework.

Q: What did the referee call when the quarterback threw a pig downfield?

A: Illegal use of hams.

Q: What sport do honeybees play?

A: Bees-ball.

Q: What does your teacher call if you run your sentences together and never use periods or commas?

A: Illegal use of ands.

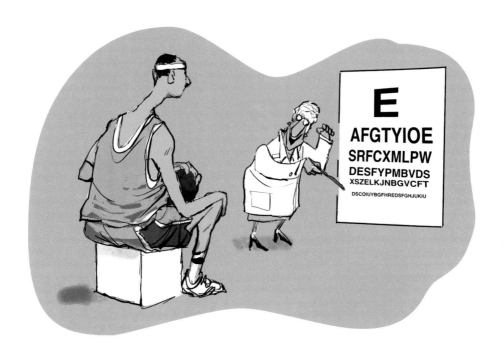

Q: What basketball team has good eyesight?

A: The Los Angeles Lookers.

Q: When office workers play football, what do they get called for?

A: Paper clipping.

Q: What do punters wear?

A: Punt-aloons.

Q: How do you catch the Atlanta Hawks?

A: In the New Jersey Nets.

Q: What do you get if you swallow a basketball?

A: A bally-ache.

Q: When do basketball players go to the beach?

A: At high tide.

Q: What's colorful, light, and floats gracefully over a baseball field?

A: A batter-fly.

Q: What end does the quarterback look at before the ball is hiked?

A: The rear end.

Q: Why did the poor quarterback have his receivers cross at midfield?

A: Because he was trying to make ends meet.

Q: What do centers wear on their feet?

A: Hiking shoes.

Q: What do frogs like to do with pins?

A: Pop flies.

Q: What do you get if you swallow a basketball hoop?

A: Hoop-atitis.

Q: Why did Dracula go to the baseball game?

A: So he could play with the bats.

Q: What did the referee call when the defense turned the quarterback into hamburger?

A: Intentional grinding.

Q: Why do football players wear face masks?

A: So they'll be ready for Halloween.

Q: What football team eats breakfast on the beach?

A: The Sandy Eggo Chargers.

Q: Why do football players wear helmets on their heads?

A: Because that's the only place they fit.

Q: Why did the referee blow the whistle on Christopher Columbus?

A: Because he was traveling.

Q: What's in the middle of a foot-bull game?

A: Calf-time.

Q: Which baseball players put curses on their opponents?

A: The Montreal Hex-pos.

Q: What kind of shots do the Hawks take?

A: Flew shots.

Q: What sport do astronauts play?

A: Space-ball.

Q: Where do the Hawks like to stand?

A: At the fowl line.

Q: What do baseball players do on Halloween?

A: They practice pitch-craft.

Q: What football player has very strong legs and builds houses?

A: A car-punter.

Q: Why did the referee call a penalty on the car-punter?

A: For roofing the passer.

Q: What's the difference between a fast base runner and a jewel thief?

A: One steals one base at a time, while the other steals the whole diamond.

Q: What do you call a baseball player who throws a tantrum?

A: A baseball brat.

Q: How are three balls and two strikes like Dracula after dinner?

A: They're both full counts.

Q: Why do batters spend a lot of time at playgrounds?

A: Because they like to swing.

Q: What do you get if you play football with long hair?

A: Split ends.

Q: What do you get if you drop an atomic bomb on a basketball court?

A: Nuclear foul out.

Q: Why did the base runner feel like garbage?

A: Because he got thrown out.

Q: Why do barbers make bad football players?

A: Because they keep clipping.

Q: What football player should you be suspicious of?

A: The quarterback sneak.

Q: Why do basketball players look at the shot clock?

A: To see how much time they've killed.

Q: What makes the Milwaukee Buicks run?

A: The Detroit Pistons.

Q: What sport do undertakers like to play?

A: Casket-ball.

Q: What kind of fence protects
quarterbacks?

A: An off-fence.

Q: Who roots for the players who sit on
the bench?

A: The chair-leaders.

Q: How do you keep a football field flat?

A: With gridirons.

Q: Who turns the lights on and off at the ballpark?

A: The switch-hitter.

Q: Where do quarterbacks go when they get old?

A: Out to pass-ture.

Q: What's the difference between a bat and a battery.

A: One can make the hit, while the other can make the heat.

Q: Which basketball players have nice lawns?

A: The Los Angeles Rakers.

Q: When soldiers play basketball, what happens when they lose?

A: They're court-martialed.

Q: What kind of dishes do baseball players have?

A: Home plates.

Q: What do quarterbacks do when they're dizzy?

A: They pass out.

Q: Why was the basketball player arrested?

A: Because he stole a ball and shot a basket.

Q: Where was the arrested player taken?

A: To the basketball court.

Q: What football game do cats like to watch?

A: The Goldfish Bowl.

Q: Where do batters go after they strike out?

A: To the outhouse.

Q: What does the referee call if a football player throws a chicken at the other team?

A: Illegal use of hens.

Q: How did the police think the basketball player died?

A: They suspected foul play.

Q: Why didn't the baseball club hire a janitor?

A: Because they already had a good cleanup hitter.

Q: Why did the pitcher decide to become a matador instead?

A: Because he had spent so many years in the bullpen.

Q: Why did the baseball player practice milking cows?

A: Because he heard he was being sent to a farm team.

Q: What do receivers catch after racing downfield?

A: They catch their breath.

Q: What's long and scaly and flies end over end down a football field?

A: A sea ser-punt.

Q: What team did the prince want to be on?

A: The Sacramento Kings.

Q: What are the Kings best at doing?

A: Holding court.

Q: What did the center do when he became a King?

A: He acted high and mighty.

Q: Why won't the army draft baseball players?

A: Because the players might steal the bases.

Q: What do you become if you get caught stealing a base?

A: An outlaw.

Q: What instrument do defensive tackles like to play?

A: The sack-sophone.

Q: If you want to sack the Dolphins' quarterback, what should you use?

A: Your fishing tackle.

Q: What's the difference between a good pitcher and a prison warden?

A: One shuts people out, while the other shuts people in.

Q: What does the referee call if the field is attacked by fish?

A: Bass interference.

Q: What should you call a basketball star?

A: Your highness.

Q: Who eats football players as they run downfield?

A: The 50-yard lion.

Q: Which baseball players will bite you if you try to run around the bases?

A: The New York Mutts.

Q: What do basketball stars sign autographs with?

A: Basketball-point pens.

Q: Where do basketball players go sailing?

A: On the high seas.

Q: What do you call an unbelievable story about a basketball player?

A: A tall tale.

Q: Why did Dorothy and Toto stay away from Detroit and Chicago?

A: Because of the Lions and Tigers and Bears, oh my!

Q: Who is the meanest person in baseball?

A: The pinch hitter.

Q: Why are the longest sports articles about pitchers?

A: Because a pitcher's worth a thousand words.

Q: Who is the most famous college running back of all time?

A: The Hunchback of Notre Dame.

Q: What's seven feet tall, plays serious basketball, and pulls everything toward it?

A: The center of gravity.

Q: Which baseball players want to be dentists?

A: The New York Yankers.

Q: If you want to play basketball on the ocean, what do you need?

A: A courtship.

Q: And who do you need on your team?

A: A coast guard.

Q: Why does everyone respect a referee when he places the football for the next down?

A: Because he lays it on the line.

Q: Why is a bad offensive lineman like a baby away from home?

A: Because they both miss their blocks.

Q: How can you stop a basketball game?

A: Tear it from rim to rim.

Q: If a basketball court is torn from rim to rim, can it be fixed?

A: No. It's hoop-less.

Q: What do you call a lineman's kids?

A: Chips off the old blocker.

Q: What's the difference between a quarterback and a baby?

A: One takes the snap, while the other takes a nap.

Q: Why are baseballs white?

A: Because they keep getting hit into the bleachers.

Q: Why did the baseball coach buy a big broom?

A: Because he wanted to sweep the World Series.

Q: Why did the frog go to the baseball game?

A: To catch fly balls.

Q: Why are city kids stronger than professional quarterbacks?

A: Because quarterbacks pass footballs once a week, but city kids pass tall buildings every day.

Q: What's red and white and black all over?

A: The Red Sox playing the White Sox at night.

Q: Who plays baseball in your living room?

A: The home team.

Q: How do you get to the Phoenix Suns?

A: With the Houston Rockets.

Q: What do receivers catch when they're tired?

A: Some Z's.

Q: What basketball team specializes in driving to the basket?

A: The Milwaukee Buicks.

Q: What do pitchers sign their contracts with?

A: Bullpens.

Q: Which football team cooks gourmet meals together?

A: The Kansas City Chefs.

Q: How fast was the basketball player running when she knocked over a player on the other team?

A: At foul speed.

This book is available in two editions:
Library binding by Carolrhoda Books, Inc.,
    a division of Lerner Publishing Group
Soft cover by First Avenue Editions,
    an imprint of Lerner Publishing Group
241 First Avenue North
Minneapolis, MN 55401 U.S.A.

Website address: www.carolrhoda.com

Library of Congress Cataloging-in-Publication Data

Walton, Rick.
    Foul play : jokes that won't strike out / by Rick and Ann Walton ; pictures by
Brian Gable.
        p.   cm. — (Make me laugh!)
    Summary: A collection of jokes about sports.
    ISBN: 1–57505–666–6 (lib. bdg. : alk. paper)
    ISBN: 1–57505–736–0 (pbk. : alk. paper)
    1. Sports—Juvenile humor. 2. Wit and humor, Juvenile. [1. Sports—Humor.
2. Jokes. 3. Riddles.] I. Walton, Ann, 1963– II. Gable, Brian, 1949– ill. III. Title.
IV. Series.
PN6231.S65W35 2005
818'.5402—dc22   2003019358

Manufactured in the United States of America
1 2 3 4 5 6 – DP – 10 09 08 07 06 05